Mini Artist **Papercraft**

Contents

See pages 2-3 for materials, equipment and hints and tips on getting started.

Getting Started

The projects in this book use lots of art materials that you will already have at home. Any missing materials can be found in art and stationery shops.

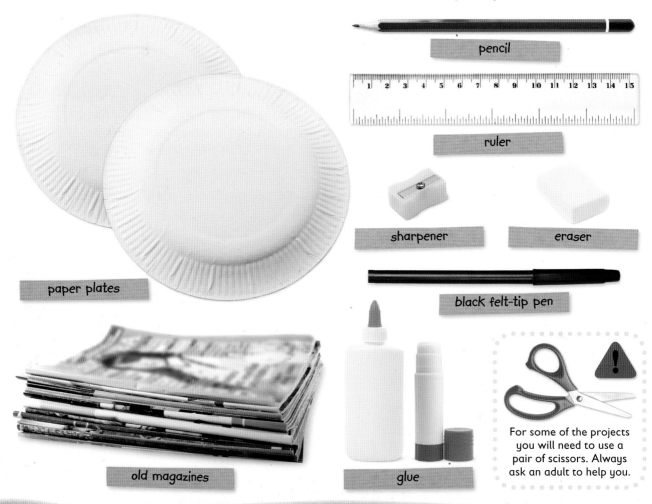

pencil

ruler

sharpener

eraser

black felt-tip pen

paper plates

old magazines

glue

For some of the projects you will need to use a pair of scissors. Always ask an adult to help you.

silver foil

books

Handy Hint

Wrapping paper, newspaper, or pieces of old wallpaper are excellent for papercraft projects. Why not start a collection?

Here is a selection of the paper you will need to complete all the papercraft projects.

House on a Hill

This pretty house is a fun project to make. You'll need coloured paper, glue and a pair of scissors.

1 Start with a piece of blue paper for the background. Cut a green strip of paper into the shape of bushes.

2 Add some pale green paper under the bushes. The pale green paper will be the grass in your picture.

3 Cut a yellow square for the house and a red triangle for the roof. Now glue all of the pieces down.

4 Cut two rectangles of red paper. Glue one to the roof for a chimney and use the other to make the door.

5 Cut two small squares from some blue paper and glue these onto the front of the house for windows.

6 Add some trees, flowers, grass and clouds in the sky to finish your picture.

Fancy Fish

To make this exciting underwater picture you will need coloured paper, glue and a pair of scissors.

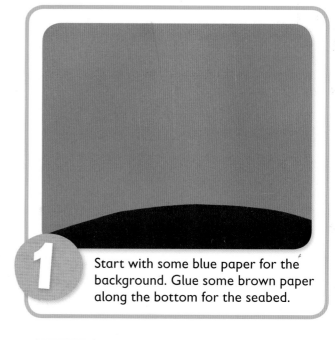

1 Start with some blue paper for the background. Glue some brown paper along the bottom for the seabed.

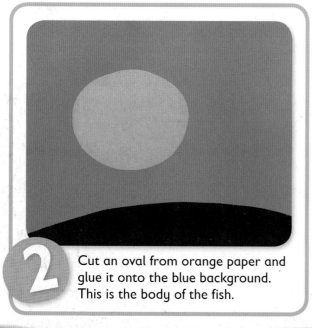

2 Cut an oval from orange paper and glue it onto the blue background. This is the body of the fish.

3 Cut some more shapes from the orange paper for the tail and fins. Glue these onto the body.

4 Now use a circle of white paper and smaller circle of black paper to make the eye. Glue them into position.

5 Cut long strips of green paper for reeds in the water. You can add red paper stripes to the body.

6 Finish your picture by adding more fish and gluing on some blue circles for bubbles.

Time for a Party

You can make these fun cards for your friends using card, coloured paper, felt-tip pens and scissors.

1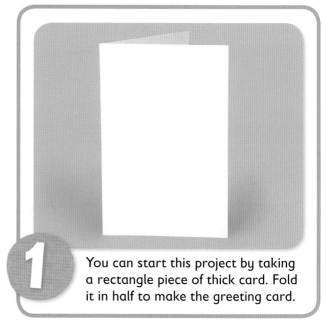

You can start this project by taking a rectangle piece of thick card. Fold it in half to make the greeting card.

2

Cut coloured balloon shapes from paper and glue them onto the card. Try to have them overlapping.

3

Use a felt-tip pen to draw a wiggly line from each balloon. These lines are the strings tied to the balloons.

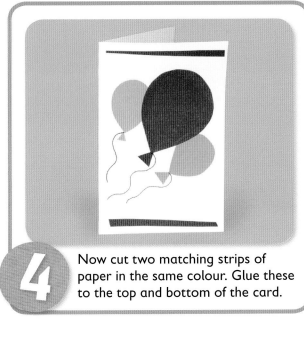

4 Now cut two matching strips of paper in the same colour. Glue these to the top and bottom of the card.

5 Use a felt-tip pen to write a message onto the front of your card. Try to do this in your best handwriting.

6 You can make fun greeting cards for all occasions using this papercraft technique.

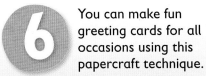

Papery City

To make this picture you will need patterned, coloured and graph paper, glue and a felt-tip pen.

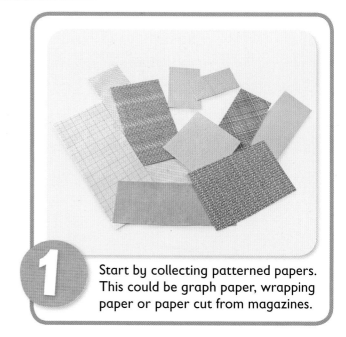

1 Start by collecting patterned papers. This could be graph paper, wrapping paper or paper cut from magazines.

2 Use a blue sheet of paper for the background. Glue a grey strip of paper to the bottom edge.

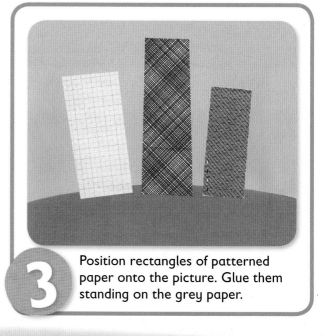

3 Position rectangles of patterned paper onto the picture. Glue them standing on the grey paper.

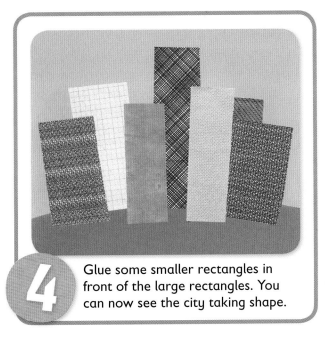

4 Glue some smaller rectangles in front of the large rectangles. You can now see the city taking shape.

5 Glue some smaller rectangles right at the very front of the picture. These are the smallest buildings.

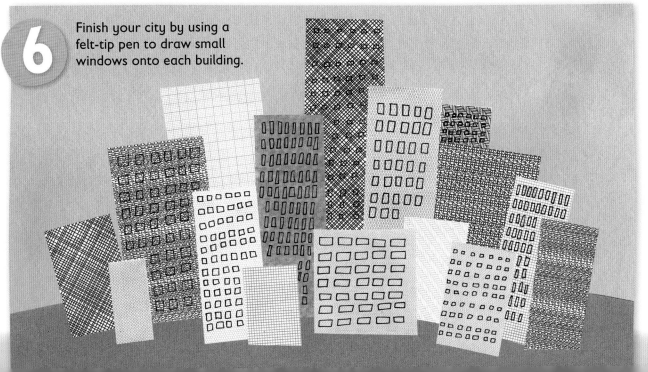

6 Finish your city by using a felt-tip pen to draw small windows onto each building.

Lovely Trees

This collage uses pictures cut from magazines. To make it, you also need coloured paper and glue.

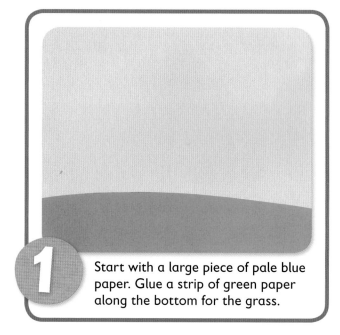

1 Start with a large piece of pale blue paper. Glue a strip of green paper along the bottom for the grass.

2 Cut three rectangles from a brown picture in a magazine. Glue them onto the picture for tree trunks.

3 Use green and yellow pictures cut from magazines to create the leaves of the trees. Glue them into position.

4 Cut grass shapes from a green magazine picture and glue these onto the green paper background.

5 Now you can cut some circles of red paper and glue these onto each of the trees to look like apples.

6 To finish your picture, you could glue some birds in nests onto the tree tops.

Mighty Mover

To make this exciting tractor scene, you will need scissors, coloured paper and some glue.

1 Start with a large piece of blue paper. Glue a strip of green paper along the bottom for the grass.

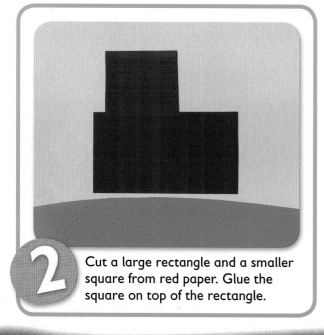

2 Cut a large rectangle and a smaller square from red paper. Glue the square on top of the rectangle.

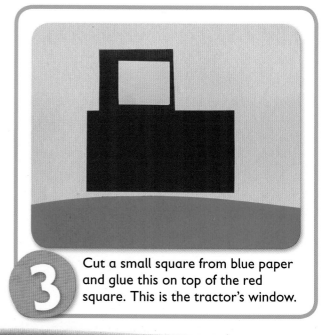

3 Cut a small square from blue paper and glue this on top of the red square. This is the tractor's window.

4 Glue two dark circles of different sizes onto the tractor for wheels. Add smaller light grey circles on top.

5 Add two strips of black paper, one for the roof and the other as the exhaust pipe. Glue them into place.

6 Finish your picture by adding a little sheep, some clouds in the sky and a barn.

Monster Mask

To make this mask, you will need a paper plate, glue, tissue paper, scissors and a felt-tip pen.

1 Use a felt-tip pen to draw a monster's face onto a paper plate. Remember to add some big fangs!

2 Rip strips of green tissue paper and glue them onto the mask. Make sure that the strips overlap each other.

3 When the mask is covered in tissue paper, use a felt-tip pen to trace over the monster's face so it is bold.

4 Ask an adult to cut out the eyes. Glue on white paper fangs and colour in the eyebrows and nostrils.

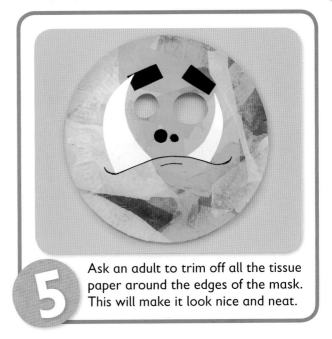

5 Ask an adult to trim off all the tissue paper around the edges of the mask. This will make it look nice and neat.

6 Use this technique to make lots of masks. Try using other shapes and colours to create new monsters.

Funky Cover

These colourful book covers are fun to make. You will need coloured paper, scissors and glue.

1 Take a large piece of coloured paper and cut it into a large rectangle that can be wrapped around your book.

2 Fold the coloured paper around the front of the book and tuck the edges inside the front and back cover.

3 Now cut a rectangle from black paper. Make sure that it is slightly smaller than the front of the book.

4 Now you can cut the black rectangle into four separate strips and glue them onto the front of the cover.

5 The next thing to do is to decorate the four stripes. Try using coloured triangles to create this zig-zag effect.

6 Why not design some more book covers? Try gluing circles on top of each other to get a different look.

Arty Frames

To make these arty frames, you will need glue, cardboard, coloured paper, silver foil and scissors.

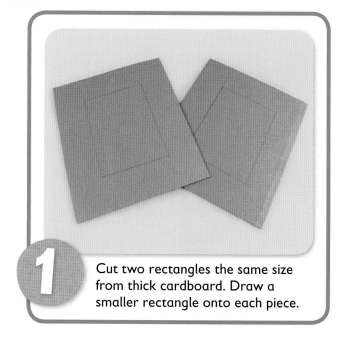

1 Cut two rectangles the same size from thick cardboard. Draw a smaller rectangle onto each piece.

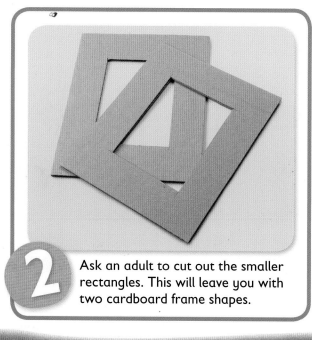

2 Ask an adult to cut out the smaller rectangles. This will leave you with two cardboard frame shapes.

3 Cut out shapes of flowers and leaves from the left-over card. You will need four flowers and eight leaves.

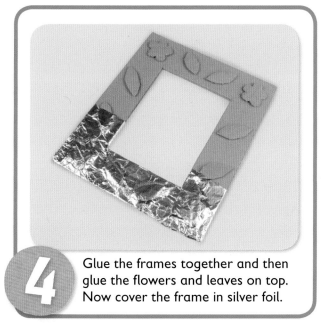

4 Glue the frames together and then glue the flowers and leaves on top. Now cover the frame in silver foil.

5 When the frame is covered in silver foil, you can add coloured paper on top of the flowers and leaf shapes.

6 Use this technique to make different frames. You could decorate frames with different coloured shapes.

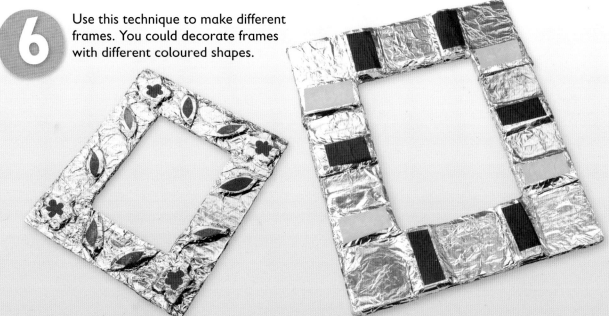

Garden Flowers

This garden flower is easy to make. You will need a pair of scissors, glue and coloured paper.

1 Start with a large piece of pale blue paper for the sky. Glue a strip of green paper for the grass.

2 Tear strips of white paper and glue them onto the blue background. They will become clouds in the sky.

3 Cut a thin strip of green paper to make the stem of the flower. Carefully glue this stem into place.